A Camera to Hold

by Jeri Cipriano

Table of Contents

Chapter 1 How Do People Take Pictures?....2

Chapter 2 What Did George Eastman Do?...6

Chapter 3 What Are Cameras Like Today?..12

Glossary/Index 15

Comprehension Check 16

Chapter 1

How Do People Take Pictures?

A friend wants to take your picture, so she says, "Say cheese." You look at the **camera** and then she clicks the button on the camera. It's all very simple.

But long ago, taking a picture wasn't that easy. If you wanted someone to take your picture, you had to sit still for half an hour!

⊙ Cameras today are very small and simple to use.

Long ago, taking pictures was hard work for the **photographer**. Cameras were very heavy machines. They were hard to hold or carry. Cameras often weighed more than 50 pounds and usually rested on three-legged stands.

⊙ The photographer took a long time to set up the equipment.

Photography in the 1860s

This photographer traveled from town to town. After he took a picture, he printed the photograph in a dark place.

At that time, there was no **film** either. Pictures were taken on heavy glass plates. The plates had to be kept in the dark, or the photographer could not print photographs from them.

Chapter 2

What Did George Eastman Do?

Some people thought that there had to be a better and easier way to take pictures. George Eastman found that way.

By 1884, film had been invented. Now a picture could be captured on film, instead of on a glass plate. Soon George Eastman made a discovery. He figured out how to make a roll of film.

☝ Eastman named his camera "Kodak" because he liked the letter K.

Then in 1888, Eastman invented a small box camera that weighed only one pound. The camera could be carried and used anywhere. And the most amazing thing was that the film went round and round on rollers inside.

Eastman made taking pictures better for everyone. His new camera was light enough for people to take with them. People would be able to take pictures everywhere they went.

Eastman was excited about these new cameras, and he wanted people to buy them. He placed an ad in the newspaper. The ad said, "You press the button, we do the rest."

At first, there wasn't much interest in the box camera. But soon, the excitement grew and everyone wanted Eastman's camera.

⋔ This ad let everyone know how easy it was to use the box camera.

The box camera was a hit. But it cost $25.00. Eastman wanted to create a less expensive camera. He believed that if a camera cost less, more people could buy it. Even parents might buy their children an inexpensive camera. The question was, what kind of camera would it be?

In 1900, Eastman invented the Brownie camera that cost just $1.00. Children and grownups everywhere loved it!

↻ The Brownie camera was named after characters in children's stories.

Taking pictures was great fun! Soon people were taking pictures of their families and friends. In fact, they took pictures of just about anything!

The Camera Company

Eastman went on to develop the largest film and camera company in the world. Today the Eastman Kodak Company is still located in Rochester, New York, where Eastman had his first office.

Chapter 3

What Are Cameras Like Today?

Over the years, new cameras were invented by other people. The new cameras could do more things.

This time line shows when different kinds of cameras were first used.

Camera Time Line

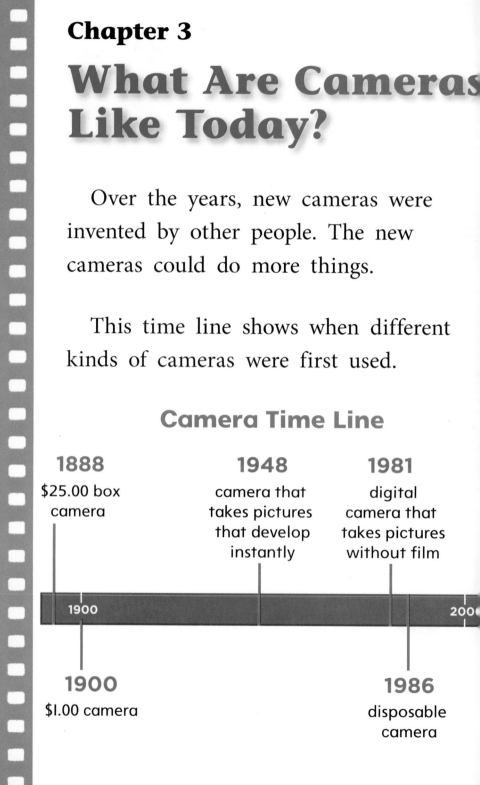

1888
$25.00 box camera

1948
camera that takes pictures that develop instantly

1981
digital camera that takes pictures without film

1900   200

1900
$1.00 camera

1986
disposable camera

⚲ This diver comes in close for a picture.

New kinds of cameras could even go underwater. Underwater photography opened a new world to everyone. Divers could take pictures of sea life that had never been seen before.

Today, there are cameras small enough to fit in your pocket. There are phone cameras and cameras that fit in a watch.

With **digital** cameras, you can see your picture before and after you take it. You can send the picture to your computer and print it yourself.

Just think how these wonderful cameras would have thrilled George Eastman.

Glossary

camera *(KAM-ruh)* something used for taking photographs *(page 2)*

digital *(DIJ-uht-uhl)* related to information in the form of numbers or digits *(page 14)*

film *(FILM)* a roll of material coated with something that makes it react to light *(page 5)*

photographer *(fuh-TAH-gruh-fuhr)* a person who takes a picture using a camera *(page 4)*

Index

Brownie, *10*

Eastman, George *6–11*, *14*

film, *5–7*

glass plates, *5, 6*

Kodak, *7, 11*

modern cameras, *12–14*

Comprehension Check

Retell

Look back at the pictures in this book. Tell a partner what you learned about cameras.

Think and Compare

1. Why did George Eastman want to make a less expensive camera than the first Kodak camera?

2. What people or things would you like to take pictures of?

3. What kinds of cameras do you think are very interesting? Why?